A Pillar Box Red Publication

in association with

ISBN: 978-1-912456-24-6

Photographs: © Getty Images. Also thanks to Craig Pugnetti, Arinsau, Fma12 and Redman19.

BARCELONA ANNUAL 2020

Written by
Jared Tinslay

Edited by
Stephen Fishlock

Designed by
Darryl Tooth

CONTENTS

SEASON REVIEW

We look back at Barça's 2018-19 campaign month by month, checking out their big moments, star players and more!

AUGUST

MEGA MOMENTS!

Vidal gets unveiled

A week before the 2018-19 season was set to kick off, Barcelona revealed their final big-name signing of the summer – CM Arturo Vidal. He joined Arthur, Malcom and Clement Lenglet as the club's fourth permanent signing of the summer transfer window!

Barça lift the Spanish Super Cup

In a change of format, the 2018 Spanish Super Cup was a one-legged game, and held outside Spain for the first time ever – in Morocco! Sevilla scored first through attacking midfielder Pablo Sarabia, but a Gerard Pique equaliser and an Ousmane Dembele stunner sealed Barça's first trophy of the season!

Los Cules' La Liga campaign started with a mega impressive win over Alaves at the Nou Camp – even though the score was 0-0 at the break. They burst into life after half-time with a Lionel Messi brace and a Philippe Coutinho goal sealing the points!

Dembele jumps for joy

MAN OF THE MONTH!

OUSMANE DEMBELE The lightning-quick France forward's long-range thunderbolt in the Spanish Super Cup v Sevilla alone would have been enough to make him Man of the Month, but he also scored the winner against Real Valladolid. Total legend!

DID YOU KNOW?

Lionel Messi's awesome free-kick opener in the win over Alaves was Barcelona's 6,000th La Liga goal of all time – he also scored their 5,000th goal against Racing Santander nine years earlier!

BARCELONA'S RESULTS

12/08	SUC	Sevilla	1-2	Barcelona
18/08	LIGA	Barcelona	3-0	Alaves
25/08	LIGA	Real Valladolid	0-1	Barcelona

SEPTEMBER

MEGA MOMENTS!

Rakuten · beko · FCB ARCELONA · 8 - 2 · MESSI (16'-42') · PULIDO pp (24') · SUAREZ (39'-90') · DEMBELE (48') · RAKITIC (52') · JORDI ALBA (81') · CUCHO (3') · ALEX GALLAR (42')

Barça thrash Huesca 8-2

La Liga minnows Huesca were in dreamland after taking a shock lead at the Nou Camp after just three minutes, but the game would end up being a total nightmare for them – Messi and Luis Suarez both scored a brace in what ended as an 8-2 thrashing!

Messi bags a free-kick v PSV

There was some more Messi magic in Barcelona's Champions League opener v Dutch giants PSV – he scored a hat-trick as Los Cules sent out a worrying message to the rest of the teams in their group!

Unfortunately, not every mega moment in 2018-19 was positive, and Barça's shock loss to bottom-of-the-table Leganes was anything but good news! It was their first defeat of the season, and let Real Madrid go level on points with them!

Leganes upset Barça

MAN OF THE MONTH!

LIONEL MESSI As well as two goals and two epic assists against Huesca, a net-buster v Girona and that Champions League hat-trick, Leo also assisted for Munir against Bilbao to help Barcelona avoid their first home defeat for more than two years!

DID YOU KNOW?

Barcelona's defeat to Leganes was only their second in La Liga under Ernesto Valverde in 43 matches!

BARCELONA'S RESULTS

Date	Comp	Home	Score	Away
02/09	LIGA	Barcelona	8-2	Huesca
15/09	LIGA	Real Sociedad	1-2	Barcelona
18/09	UCL	Barcelona	4-0	PSV
23/09	LIGA	Barcelona	2-2	Girona
26/09	LIGA	Leganes	2-1	Barcelona
29/09	LIGA	Barcelona	1-1	Athletic Bilbao

OCTOBER

MEGA MOMENTS!

Barcelona outclass Tottenham

It took just two minutes for Philippe Coutinho to score the opener for Barcelona against Tottenham in the Champo League, but the star of the show was Messi yet again – he scored twice and hit the post another two times as they brushed Spurs aside!

BARCELONA'S RESULTS

Date	Comp	Home	Score	Away
03/10	UCL	Tottenham	2-4	Barcelona
07/10	LIGA	Valencia	1-1	Barcelona
20/10	LIGA	Barcelona	4-2	Sevilla
24/10	UCL	Barcelona	2-0	Inter
28/10	LIGA	Barcelona	5-1	Real Madrid
31/10	CDR	Cultural Leonesa	0-1	Barcelona

Barça went into their game against Sevilla in third, just one place behind their opponents, and on a poor four-game league winless run. There was good news and bad news for Los Cules – they put four past Sevilla, but Messi fractured his arm!

Messi writhes in pain

Without Messi, Barça supporters were well nervous going into their match against arch rivals Real Madrid, but striker Luis Suarez stepped up to the plate big time with a hat-trick – and Real manager Julen Lopetegui was sacked a day later!

Suarez hits a treble

MAN OF THE MONTH!

LUIS SUAREZ We were really tempted to give the award to Coutinho after he netted three goals in October, but how could we look past the star that scored a hat-trick against the club's fiercest rivals?

DID YOU KNOW?

October's El Clasico was the first in nearly 11 years not to feature either Lionel Messi or Cristiano Ronaldo!

NOVEMBER

MEGA MOMENTS!

Suarez reels off in celebration

Barcelona were 2-1 down with just four minutes of normal time to play against Rayo Vallecano, but two last-gasp goals from Ousmane Dembele and Luis Suarez sealed a proper dramatic comeback to send them four points clear at the top of the table!

BARCELONA'S RESULTS

03/11	LIGA	Rayo Vallecano	2-3	Barcelona
06/11	UCL	Inter	1-1	Barcelona
11/11	LIGA	Barcelona	3-4	Real Betis
24/11	LIGA	Atletico Madrid	1-1	Barcelona
28/11	UCL	PSV	1-2	Barcelona

The Champo League game v Inter was a landmark moment for two reasons – Malcom scored his first competitive goal for the club just minutes after coming on as a substitute, and Barcelona sealed qualification for the knockout stages of the CL!

Malcom gets off the mark

MAN OF THE MONTH!

OUSMANE DEMBELE The supersub came off the bench against Rayo Vallecano and Atletico Madrid, scoring crucial late goals in both games, then set Lionel Messi up for his jaw-dropping strike v PSV!

DID YOU KNOW?

Messi scored twice on his return to action against Real Betis following injury, but Barça still lost their first league home game since September 2016!

DECEMBER

MEGA MOMENTS!

After scraping a league draw in 2017-18 at city rivals Espanyol's stadium, and losing in the Copa del Rey there, Barça fans were nervous ahead of their short trip – but they needn't have been! Messi scored TWO free-kicks to help seal an easy derby win!

Messi finds the target once again

BARCELONA'S RESULTS

02/12	LIGA	Barcelona	2-0	Villarreal
05/12	CDR	Barcelona	4-1	Cultural Leonesa
08/12	LIGA	Espanyol	0-4	Barcelona
11/12	UCL	Barcelona	1-1	Tottenham
16/12	LIGA	Levante	0-5	Barcelona
22/12	LIGA	Barcelona	2-0	Celta Vigo

'El Pistolero' fires in another goal

It was Levante that stopped Barcelona from going the whole of 2017-18 unbeaten, but La Blaugrana got their revenge in December 2018! Messi scored a hat-trick, and his 50th goal for club and country in 2018, while Suarez and Pique also busted net!

MAN OF THE MONTH!

LIONEL MESSI Two direct free-kicks in one La Liga game was a first for Leo, then he went and topped it by scoring an amazing treble against Levante! The Argentine went into the winter break with 15 La Liga goals – more than any other player!

DID YOU KNOW?

Carles Alena scored his first ever La Liga goal for Barcelona with a dinked finish against Villarreal!

JANUARY

MEGA MOMENTS!

Suarez bagged a brace against Eibar, but Messi grabbed the headlines after scoring his 400th La Liga goal! He became the first player ever to score 400 league goals for a single club in Europe's top five leagues too. Hero!

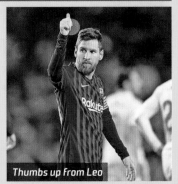
Thumbs up from Leo

After their shock first-leg defeat to Levante in the Copa del Rey last 16 tie, La Blaugrana came back at the Nou Camp with a double from Dembele – both assisted by Messi – and then another goal from Leo himself!

Dembele fires home

Barça needed another dramatic second-leg comeback in the Copa del Rey quarter-final against Sevilla. Philippe Coutinho was the hero at the Nou Camp, as he scored twice in a 6-1 hammering and put in his best display in an up-and-down season!

Coutinho celebrates

BARCELONA'S RESULTS

06/01	LIGA	Getafe	1-2	Barcelona
10/01	CDR	Levante	2-1	Barcelona
13/01	LIGA	Barcelona	3-0	Eibar
17/01	CDR	Barcelona	3-0	Levante
20/01	LIGA	Barcelona	3-1	Leganes
23/01	CDR	Sevilla	2-0	Barcelona
27/01	LIGA	Girona	0-2	Barcelona
30/01	CDR	Barcelona	6-1	Sevilla

MAN OF THE MONTH!

LIONEL MESSI The only two games Messi didn't play, Barcelona lost – and every game Leo played, he scored! His stoppage-time goal against Sevilla at the end of the month was the eighth consecutive match that he'd netted in all comps. What a ledge!

DID YOU KNOW?

Kevin Prince-Boateng made his debut for Barcelona in the 2-0 Copa del Rey first-leg defeat to Sevilla!

FEBRUARY

MEGA MOMENTS!

Ter Stegen makes a worldy save

Barcelona drew Lyon in the last 16 of the Champions League, but they fired a blank in the first leg at the Groupama Stadium. Keeper Marc-Andre ter Stegen pulled off one of the saves of the campaign to keep out Martin Terrier's drive!

Deadly double act

Back in La Liga, Sevilla stunned Barça by scoring the opener, but a Messi masterclass turned things on its head! He levelled with a wicked volley, curled in a second and then chipped the GK to seal his 50th career hat-trick, before assisting Suarez for the fourth. Wow!

After drawing at the Nou Camp earlier in the month in the Copa del Rey semi-final first leg, Barcelona smashed Real Madrid 3-0 at the Santiago Bernabeu to reach their sixth straight cup final!

Barça sink Real Madrid

BARCELONA'S RESULTS

02/02	LIGA	Barcelona	2-2	Valencia
06/02	CDR	Barcelona	1-1	Real Madrid
10/02	LIGA	Athletic Bilbao	0-0	Barcelona
16/02	LIGA	Barcelona	1-0	Real Valladolid
19/02	UCL	Lyon	0-0	Barcelona
23/02	LIGA	Sevilla	2-4	Barcelona
27/02	CDR	Real Madrid	0-3	Barcelona

MAN OF THE MONTH!

MARC-ANDRE TER STEGEN The class Germany keeper made two fine saves to deny Bilbao victory in La Liga, was heroic in their CL game v Lyon and kept another two clean sheets v Real Madrid and Real Valladolid to cap off an awesome month!

DID YOU KNOW?

Gerard Pique became the seventh superstar to play 100 CL games for Barça when they took on Lyon!

MARCH

MEGA MOMENTS!

Rakitic scores

Bragging rights were well and truly with Barcelona supporters after they bagged a second El Clasico win in four days at the Santiago Bernabeu, thanks to an Ivan Rakitic goal. It also put Los Cules ten points clear at the top of the table!

Back in the Champions League, and Barcelona rediscovered their shooting boots against Lyon – they made up for not scoring in the first leg by busting net five times in front of their home fans to qualify for the quarter-finals!

Pique salutes the crowd

Leo's the hero once more

Jaws well and truly dropped when Barcelona travelled to Betis' stadium – Messi scored a mind-boggling hat-trick, including a spectacular free-kick and an outrageous one-touch chipped finish from the edge of the penalty area!

MAN OF THE MONTH!

LIONEL MESSI It's that man again! He bagged 11 goals and assists combined in just five games, including a double against city rivals Espanyol, to ensure Barça were still ten points clear at the end of the month and heading into a CL quarter-final!

DID YOU KNOW?

Barcelona's win over Real Madrid was their 96th El Clasico victory overall, putting them ahead in head-to-heads for the first time in 87 years!

BARCELONA'S RESULTS

Date	Comp	Home	Score	Away
02/03	LIGA	Real Madrid	0-1	Barcelona
09/03	LIGA	Barcelona	3-1	Rayo Vallecano
13/03	UCL	Barcelona	5-1	Lyon
17/03	LIGA	Real Betis	1-4	Barcelona
30/03	LIGA	Barcelona	2-0	Espanyol

APRIL

MEGA MOMENTS!

It's pure joy for Suarez

With eight games left to play and eight points separating them in the table, Barça's clash with second-placed Atletico was essentially a title decider. Diego Costa was sent off after 28 minutes, but it wasn't until the 85th minute that Suarez broke the deadlock – and Messi scored a minute later!

Coutinho's screamer

Luke Shaw's own goal at Old Trafford handed Los Cules a slender lead going into their CL quarter-final second leg v Man. United. A brace from Leo Messi, plus a Coutinho wondergoal, put the tie to bed and took Barça to their first CL semi-final since 2015!

A second-half goal against Levante from… yep, you guessed it, Lionel Messi, sealed Barça's 26th La Liga title with three games to spare! Messi started on the bench, but beat two defenders before stroking the ball past the keeper to clinch another trophy!

Leo lifts the title

MAN OF THE MONTH!

LIONEL MESSI He hit vital goals against Villarreal and Atletico, and a blistering brace v Man. United but, most importantly, Messi scored the goal that sealed the title against Levante! Leo also became the first player to win ten league titles with Barcelona!

DID YOU KNOW?

Messi and Suarez both scored in stoppage-time to somehow salvage a 4-4 draw against Villarreal!

BARCELONA'S RESULTS

Date	Comp	Home	Score	Away
02/04	LIGA	Villarreal	4-4	Barcelona
06/04	LIGA	Barcelona	2-0	Atletico Madrid
10/04	UCL	Man. United	0-1	Barcelona
13/04	LIGA	Huesca	0-0	Barcelona
16/04	UCL	Barcelona	3-0	Man. United
20/04	LIGA	Barcelona	2-1	Real Sociedad
23/04	LIGA	Alaves	0-2	Barcelona
27/04	LIGA	Barcelona	1-0	Levante

Barcelona beat Liverpool 3-0 in the Champions League semi-final first leg

MAY

MEGA MOMENTS!

Suarez scores against his old club

The Champions League semi-final first leg against Liverpool went exactly to plan for Barça. Ex-Red Luis Suarez scored the opener before Lionel Messi netted a double, including a sensational free-kick, to give his side a massive three-goal advantage...

...but things went horribly wrong in the return leg at Anfield! Liverpool produced one of the best European comebacks of all time to win 4-0 on the night, and 4-3 on aggregate, to end La Blaugrana's Champions League dream. Ouch!

Suarez is left stunned

Messi is gutted

And the misery didn't end there. Barça were hoping to end 2018-19 with a Spanish double, but Valencia put on a superb showing to win the Copa del Rey final and stop Barcelona from winning their fifth cup final in a row!

MAN OF THE MONTH!

LIONEL MESSI It's a hat-trick of Man of the Months for magic man Messi, but he would have been happier had Barcelona reached the Champo League final and won the Copa del Rey! He still scored five goals in May, and ended the 2018-19 season with his sixth European Golden Shoe!

DID YOU KNOW?

Messi's second goal against Liverpool in the Champions League semi-final first leg at the Nou Camp brought up his 600th goal for the club. Legend!

BARCELONA'S RESULTS

01/05	UCL	Barcelona	3-0	Liverpool
04/05	LIGA	Celta Vigo	2-0	Barcelona
07/05	UCL	Liverpool	4-0	Barcelona
12/05	LIGA	Barcelona	2-0	Getafe
19/05	LIGA	Eibar	2-2	Barcelona
25/05	CDR	Barcelona	1-2	Valencia

LA LIGA CHAMPS!

Barça lifted their 26th La Liga trophy in 2018-19, so we've picked out some of the best stats behind their title-winning season...

2,535 No Blaugrana superstar completed more passes than Ivan Rakitic – he was second in the entire La Liga charts!

19 They ended the season 19 points ahead of Real Madrid – the furthest they've ever finished above their Clasico rivals in the league!

61% Barcelona bossed 61.4% possession on average in La Liga – they were the only team to average over 60%!

8 They won eight games in a row between December and January – another record for 2018-19!

23 Barça also went on an epic 23-league game unbeaten run in 2018-19 – the longest of any La Liga team!

93,265

The biggest La Liga attendance of the season turned out to watch Barcelona thrash Real Madrid 5-1 at the Nou Camp!

36

Lionel Messi scored 36 goals – his fifth-best tally in a single La Liga season – to win the top scorer prize for the sixth time!

13

No player got more La Liga assists than the Argentina superstar either!

6

Classy Chile midfielder Arturo Vidal was the player who provided the most assists for Messi!

WORDFIT

Fit the awesome Barcelona academy products into this grid!

Alba ✓	Deulofeu ✓	Jony ✓	Pedro	Roberto ✓
Alena ✓	Dos Santos	Messi ✓	Pique ✓	Romeu ✓
Bartra ✓	Fabregas ✓	Montoya	Puyol ✓	Thiago ✓
Bojan ✓	Guardiola	Munir	Rafinha ✓	Valdes ✓
Busquets ✓	Iniesta	Navarro ✓	Reina ✓	Xavi ✓

SPOT THE DIFFERENCE

Study these Barcelona v Getafe pictures really carefully, then see if you can find the ten differences between them!

ANSWERS ON PAGE 60

NOU CAMP IN PICS

Check out these behind-the-scenes snaps of Barça's sick stadium!

There's a statue of legendary ex-striker Laszlo Kubala outside the ground!

There's a small chapel beside the tunnel leading to the Nou Camp pitch!

FACTFILE

Built: 1957

Capacity: 99,354

Nearest Neighbour: Espanyol

First Match: Barcelona 4-2 Warsaw, 1957

Record Attendance: 120,000 v Juventus, 1986

The home dressing room is painted in La Blaugrana's famous colours...

...whereas the away changing room is a much more basic white!

The Nou Camp is being renovated soon – by 2023-24, it will have a new capacity of around 105,000!

The teams walk down this long stairway tunnel before they're greeted by the fans!

There's a museum inside the ground too, with trophies and interactive screens!

GRIEZMANN

LES BLEUS BALLER

The France forward's arrival at Barça has been a long time coming!

'Trains don't come around just once', were the wise words of lethal La Liga goal machine Antoine Griezmann after he joined Barcelona in July 2019. Just over twelve months earlier, the France World Cup winner had rejected Barça's advances to stay at Atletico Madrid for another season – confirming his highly-anticipated decision through a famous televised documentary called 'The Decision'. He obviously regretted making that choice though, and ended up telling Atletico Madrid chiefs at the end of the 2018-19 campaign that he wanted to leave – with La Blaugrana willing to go back in for him. Barça paid his massive £107 million release clause, handed him a five-year contract and stuck a new £717 million buy-out clause on his head – higher than any other Barcelona superstar ever, including Lionel Messi!

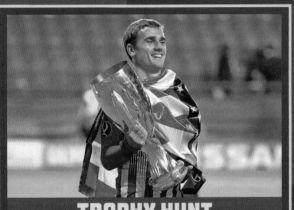

TROPHY HUNT

In Griezmann, Barça knew they were signing a player with tons of La Liga experience and success – he finished as Atletico's top scorer in all five of his seasons at the club and was named the Spanish league's Best Player in 2016! He lifted some silverware with Atletico, but never got his hands on La Liga, the Copa del Rey or Champions League, so he'll be desperate to win those with La Blaugrana!

THE URUGUAYAN

Grizi won the World Cup with France, but his nickname is actually 'The Uruguayan'! As well as loving the culture of the South American country, plus its famous Mate tea, he's also had a helping hand from the nation throughout his career. He was given his Real Sociedad debut by coach Martin Lasarte, was big buddies with ex-Atletico hero Diego Godin and now he's playing alongside Luis Suarez!

MADRID MAULER

The good news for Barcelona is that Griezmann has an amazing scoring record against arch rivals Real Madrid! Before the 2019-20 season, he'd scored eight net-busters against Los Blancos – only netting more goals against two other La Liga sides. With a further five assists and wins against them in both UEFA and Spanish Supercup finals, his new fans are hoping his Real-busting run continues!

BASKETBALL BARMY

If you follow Antoine on social media you'll already know this, but he's a huge basketball fanatic – he even had a basketball court in his old house in Madrid to practise on! His favourite player is Derrick Rose of the Detroit Pistons, but we get the feeling he loves being courtside at any NBA game. Once Grizi's finished ripping nets and hangs up his boots, a career as a basketball commentator awaits!

2018-19 LA LIGA STATS

Games: 37
Goals: 15
Assists: 9
Key Passes: 74
Shot Accuracy: 53%

AMAZING YouTube CLIPS!

Get a load of some of the coolest videos on *BARCELONA's* official YouTube channel! You have to watch these...

BARCELONA QR CODES EXPLAINED

This is a QR code – just scan it with your phone or tablet to watch each video clip on YouTube. Here's how to do it:

 Download and install a free QR Code reader from the app or android store.

 Hold your phone or tablet over the QR code and you'll be sent to the clip. Easy!

MY TOP 4

V. VALDES

there was always a moment in which we needed him,

1:35 / 8:12   HD

▶ Pique Picks His Heroes!

Barcelona centre-back Gerard Pique is a walking, talking Blaugrana ledge himself, but in this wicked video he picks his top four past legends to have worn the Barcelona shirt – a goalkeeper, defender, midfielder and striker! Have a watch of the clip and see if you agree with his final four choices!

▶ Barça Emojis!

You've got a crown, a rocket, a ghost and an octopus – which Emoji would you give to each member of the Barça squad? Chile's Arturo Vidal and last season's loanee Kevin Prince-Boateng gave it a go in this mega funny clip!

N.SEMEDO

We'll give Jordi this one.

1:35 / 8:12   HD

▶ #Messi10

It feels like Lionel Messi's been bossing Barça's No.10 shirt forever, but he actually took it on in his fifth season – Ronaldinho passed it down to him! Even though this vid's titled #MESSI10, it's actually a compilation of his goals when he was wearing the No.30 and No.19 jerseys!

▶ Mystery Box Madness!

Speedy forward Ousmane Dembele is awesome at skinning defenders, but he's pretty good at guessing what things are just by touching them too! The France World Cup winner had to put his hands into a mystery box and say what the objects were without seeing them!

▶ Frenkie Put To Test!

It's all good knowing everything about FC Barcelona, but you've got to know a bit about the city too – just ask summer arrival Frenkie de Jong! He was quizzed on ten things about the Catalan capital by his Netherlands team-mate Jasper Cillessen – can you beat him?

▶ La Liga Legends!

It doesn't matter how many La Liga trophies you win, you're always going to celebrate each one like mad – just ask the Barcelona players! This class behind-the-scenes video follows the superstars around the pitch as they celebrate last season's title victory at the Nou Camp!

▶ Goals, Goals, Goals!

Warning... this video contains a LOT of busted nets! The Barcelona Femeni team reached their first ever Champions League final in 2019 – and this awesome, goal-packed video shows all 18 goals they scored en route to the final. Which one is your favourite?

MESSI
50 HAT-TRICKS

Last season, BARCELONA and ARGENTINA superstar LIONEL MESSI reached a half-century of hat-tricks for club and country! We take a look at some of his best trebles for BARÇA...

Hat-Trick 1

Barcelona	3	3	Real Madrid

March 2007 Of all the teams that Messi could have chosen to score his first career hat-trick against, we reckon Real Madrid would have been top of the list! After netting two first-half strikes, but then watching Sergio Ramos head Real 3-2 ahead, a 19-year-old Leo beat two defenders and smashed a low shot into the far corner – and in the dying minutes of the game too!

Hat-Trick 2

Atletico Madrid 1 | 3 Barcelona

January 2009 Blaugrana fans had to wait just under two years for Leo's next hat-trick, but it happened to be his first in the Copa del Rey – and his first away from the Nou Camp! Barcelona went on to lift the trophy that year, with Messi bagging another goal in the final, his first Copa del Rey trophy and the Golden Boot prize!

Barcelona 4 | 1 Arsenal

April 2010 It counts as a hat-trick, but this was in fact Leo's first ever four-goal haul! It was also his first in the Champo League and first against an English side! After a 2-2 draw in the first leg, three goals in just 20 minutes totally killed the tie – Leo's first was a thunderbolt and his third a cheeky lob – before he added a fourth late on!

Hat-Trick 6

Barcelona 3 | 0 Valencia

March 2010 Let's all spare a thought for Valencia – no side has been on the receiving end of more Messi hat-tricks than 'The Bats'! Our favourite treble v them was this one from 2010 and, in particular, Leo's opening goal. He turned three defenders inside-out before giving the goalkeeper the eyes and slotting into the near post!

Hat-Trick 4

Barcelona 4 | 0 Sevilla

August 2010 Of his first 50 career hat-tricks, only one came in a final – and it ended up winning Los Cules the 2010 Spanish Super Cup! They'd lost the first leg in Seville 3-1, with Messi starting on the subs' bench, but he was in the starting line-up for the return at the Nou Camp – a decision that obviously paid off massively!

Hat-Trick 7

Barcelona	7	1	B. Leverkusen

March 2012 To say that German club Leverkusen were destroyed in this Champions League clash would be an understatement! On-fire Messi ran riot from the right wing, and became the first player in the competition's history to score five net-busters in a single match – he even chipped goalkeeper Bernd Leno twice. Class!

Hat-Trick 18

Hat-Trick 19

Barcelona	5	3	Granada

March 2012 Apart from scoring three top-quality goals, including a first-time volley and a half-volley lob, there were more important reasons for Messi to celebrate this treble! The goals took him above Barça legend Cesar Rodriguez at the top of the club's all-time top scorers' list – and he was only 24 at the time. Wow!

Barcelona	4	0	Ajax

September 2013 After watching arch-rival Cristiano Ronaldo score a sick Champions League treble for Real Madrid the night before, Leo was obviously pumped to prove that anything C-Ron could do, he could do better! He started the night with another epic free-kick, before twisting and turning his way to another two ace goals!

Barcelona	4	0	Espanyol

May 2012 As well as being another amazing four-goal haul for the Argentina legend, this one was interesting because three of the goals were from set-pieces! His first was a screamer of a free-kick, which he curled in from way outside the box, and then his second and fourth strikes were ice-cool efforts from the penalty spot!

Hat-Trick 27

Hat-Trick 21

| Real Madrid | 3 | 4 | Barcelona |

March 2014 Messi's first ever treble at the Santiago Bernabeu was mega dramatic! He'd already scored one when Ronaldo put Madrid 3-2 ahead from the spot with 35 minutes remaining. Incredibly, Barça then won two penalties themselves, with Messi holding his nerve to score both – including the winner in the 84th minute!

Hat-Trick 29

Hat-Trick 30

| Barcelona | 5 | 1 | Sevilla |

November 2014 Athletic Bilbao legend Telmo Zarra's all-time La Liga goalscoring record had stood for nearly 60 years – he hit 251 goals in 15 seasons, a record that some experts thought would never be broken! But with this hat-trick against Sevilla, Leo didn't just break the record – he bettered it in five fewer seasons. Crazy!

Hat-Trick 31

| APOEL | 0 | 4 | Barcelona |

November 2014 Messi was obviously still on a huge high after becoming La Liga's all-time record scorer, because just three days later he netted another treble! As well as overtaking Raul's all-time Champo League scoring record with this hat-trick, it was also special because it was entirely with his 'weaker' right foot!

Deportivo	0	4	Barcelona

January 2015 We've singled out this hat-trick mainly because of Messi's surprise opener – it was an absolute bullet of a header from further out than the penalty spot! His second goal was much more trademark Messi – a clever, dinked finish over the onrushing goalkeeper!

Hat-Trick 33

Hat-Trick 35

Barcelona	6	1	Rayo Vallecano

March 2015 Three goals in a 12-minute spell made this league hat-trick at the Nou Camp the quickest of Leo's entire jaw-dropping career! It also took him to 24 La Liga trebles, overtaking Cristiano Ronaldo's record and setting a new domestic landmark in the process!

Barcelona	4	0	Man. City

October 2016 A month after scoring a Champions League hat-trick against Celtic, Messi bagged another one against a British side! He became just the second player in history to score back-to-back CL trebles, and took his overall goal tally in the competition at the Nou Camp to 50 – a new home record for the tournament!

Hat-Trick 41

Hat-Trick 46

Deportivo	2	4	Barcelona

April 2018 This class hat-trick sealed the 2017-18 La Liga title for Barcelona, and also made sure that Messi moved above Liverpool's Mo Salah in the Golden Shoe standings as Europe's top goalscorer for the season! His first goal was the pick of the bunch – it was a first-time volley after a chip into the box from Luis Suarez!

ARGENTINA HAT-TRICKS!

Check out the six international trebles that helped Leo get to 50...

February 2012	
Switzerland	1
Argentina	3

84:50 HALF 2	
Argentina	4
Brazil	3

June 2013	
Guatemala	0
Argentina	4

Barcelona	4	0	PSV

September 2018 The little Barça magician couldn't have started the 2018-19 Champions League campaign any better! His first goal against Dutch giants PSV was a pinpoint free-kick into the top bins, his second was a controlled first-time volley from a lobbed pass and his hat-trick clincher was a right-footed piledriver!

Hat-Trick 48

Hat-Trick 49

Levante	0	5	Barcelona

December 2018 Just days before this game, Brazil legend Pele said Messi wasn't a match for him, and he only had one foot! On top of that, Luka Modric had just won the Ballon d'Or award and Leo didn't even make the podium. What better way to prove them wrong than with another treble – the first a perfect right-footed finish!

Sevilla	2	3	Barcelona

February 2019 Messi brought up his half-century of trebles with three eye-popping finishes! His first was a swivelling, acrobatic first-time volley from the edge of the area, his second was placed into the top corner with his right foot and his hat-trick goal was a subtle dink over the keeper from close range. Take a bow, Leo!

Hat-Trick 50

Argentina	5
Panama	0

Jun 2016

Ecuador	1
Argentina	3

Argentina	4
Haiti	0

May 2018

BARCELONA BRAIN-BUSTER!

Can you answer these teasers correctly?

1. Name the Barcelona vice-captain in the 2018-19 season!

2. True or False? No manager has won more trophies at the club than Pep Guardiola!

3. Which club did Brazil winger Malcom join Barça from in 2018 – Lille, Rennes or Bordeaux?

4. Who won the first ever El Clasico – Real Madrid or Barça?

5. What was the aggregate scoreline of both La Liga Clasicos in 2018-19?

6. What year did Ousmane Dembele join the club – 2015, 2016 or 2017?

7. Which 2018-19 goalkeeper was taller – Jasper Cillessen or Marc-Andre ter Stegen?

8. What shirt number does speedy left-back Jordi Alba wear for the Catalan club?

9. Where did Barcelona Femeni finish in the table in 2018-19 – first, second or third?

10. Who scored more goals in all competitions in 2018-19 – Ivan Rakitic or Gerard Pique?

1. Sergio Busquets
2. True
3. Bordeaux
4. Barcelona
5. FCB 5-1 RM
6. 2017
7. Ter Stegen
8. No. 18
9. Second
10. Pique

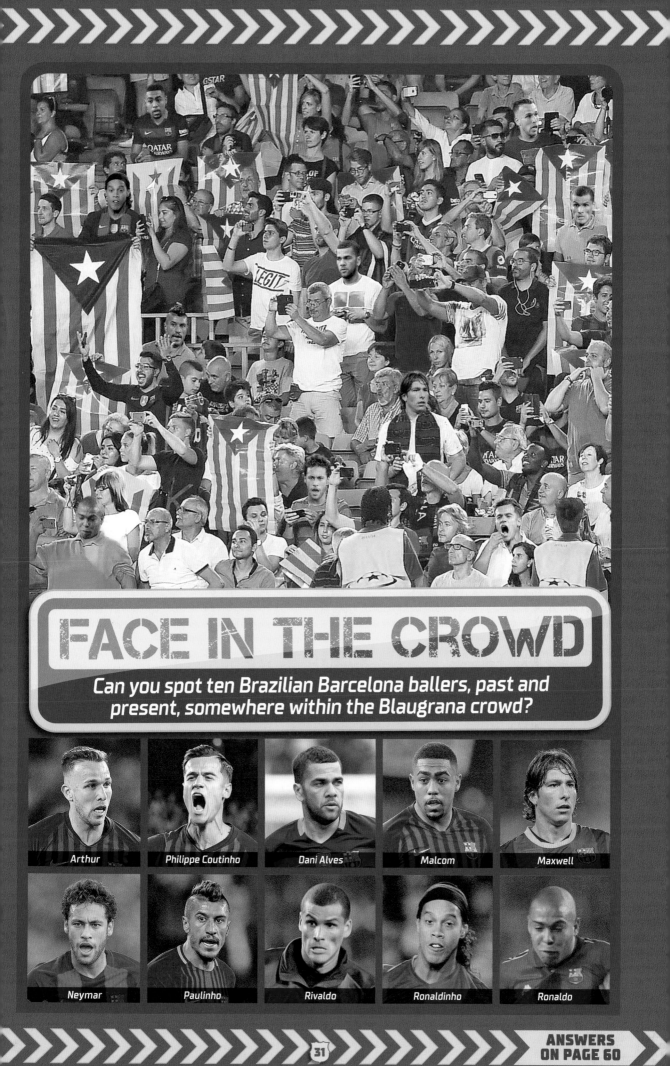

FACE IN THE CROWD

Can you spot ten Brazilian Barcelona ballers, past and present, somewhere within the Blaugrana crowd?

Arthur

Philippe Coutinho

Dani Alves

Malcom

Maxwell

Neymar

Paulinho

Rivaldo

Ronaldinho

Ronaldo

ANSWERS ON PAGE 60

BARCELONA

A

AMOR!

Amor means 'love' in Spanish, and Barcelona fans were head over heels for old central midfielder Guillermo Amor! After coming through their academy, he broke into the first team in the late '80s and ended up making over 560 appearances in a ten-year spell. By the time he left Barça, he'd won more trophies than any other player in the history of the club at the time!

B

BRAZIL!

Barcelona may be based in Spain, but in the past it's had a special connection with a country in South America – Brazil! Some incredible Samba Stars have played for the club, including Dani Alves, Ronaldinho, Neymar, Rivaldo, Romario and Ronaldo. Fans of the club have their fingers tightly crossed that Arthur can go on to make as big an impact as they did!

C

CLASICO!

Before we start this one, we should apologise – we're about to mention two very naughty words in the Barcelona dictionary... Real Madrid! The capital club are Barcelona's fiercest rivals, and their epic annual clashes are known as El Clasico. It's one of the most-watched football matches on the planet, and Barça are currently ahead on victories in the all-time head-to-heads!

A-Z

D

DECO!

Even though he played for Portugal, Deco was born in Brazil, so DNA was already on his side when he arrived at the club in 2004. He had a massive influence, too – he helped Barça win La Liga in his first season, then won the Champions League and Barcelona's Player of the Season prize in 2005-06! He eventually left as a club legend in 2008 to join Chelsea!

E

ESPANYOL!

Barcelona's biggest rivals are obviously Real Madrid, but they don't get on that well with their neighbours Espanyol either! The 'Derbi Barceloni', as it's known in the city due to the clubs' stadiums being just three miles apart, has almost 120 years of history and always has an edge to it!

G

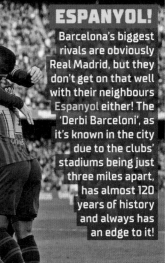

GAMPER!

Joan Gamper is probably the most important person in Barcelona's history, because it wouldn't even exist without him! The Swiss footy fan and player founded the club in 1899 after posting an advert for players in one of the city's newspapers! He played 48 games for them until 1903, scored 100 goals, then became the president in 1908!

F

FEMENI!

Since their foundation in 1988, Barcelona Femeni have become one of the most successful women's teams in Spain, with four Primera Division titles, six Copas de la Reina and nine Copas Catalunya! They play their home games at the newly-built Estadi Johan Cruyff, which holds 6,000 fans, and came second in the league in 2018-19 and were runners-up in the Champo League!

H

HYMN!

Next time you tune in to a Barcelona game on TV, take a moment to hear the fans singing the club's official hymn – or the 'Cant del Barça', as it's known in the city. They play it through the loudspeakers at the Nou Camp just before kick-off and after the final whistle at every home game, but the fans often break into song during matches as well!

I

INIESTA!

You just have to watch clips of the send-off Barcelona gave Andres Iniesta at the end of the 2017-18 season to see how much he meant to the club. The little magician came through their academy, spent 16 seasons in the senior squad – three as captain – and then left as the most decorated Spanish footballer of all time with 32 club trophies and three for Spain. Legend!

J

JOHAN CRUYFF!

Johan Cruyff is such an important part of Barcelona's history, they've even named the new stadium that will be home to Barça B and the Femeni team after him. As well as helping the club win their first La Liga title in 14 years in 1973-74 as a player, he then managed the side for eight seasons, lifting four league titles and the club's first ever European Cup in 1992!

K

KUBALA!

One player that was so good he's got a statue in honour of him at the Nou Camp is ex-striker Laszlo Kubala! During his 11-year spell at the club, he smashed in an amazing 281 goals in 357 matches, and holds the record for most goals scored in a single La Liga game – he netted seven in Barça's 9-0 win over Sporting Gijon in February 1952!

L

LOS CULES!

The letter 'L' represents Barça's cool nicknames – Los Cules and La Blaugrana. While La Blaugrana refers to the team's colours – blau means blue in Catalan, and grana means deep red – Los Cules actually translates to 'Bums'! It comes from when supporters sat on walls around the ground to see the team in action – and people walking in the street could see their bottoms from below!

M

MESSI!

When Lionel Messi made his La Liga debut back in 2004, there was a real sense of excitement, but what he's gone on to achieve is absolutely incredible! Not only is he the club's all-time top scorer, he also holds the record for most La Liga goals, busted more nets against Real Madrid than any other Barça player and lifted more trophies for the club than anyone else!

N

NOU CAMP!

The award for biggest footy stadium in Europe goes to the Nou Camp! It currently holds 99,354 fans, but plans to extend it will bump it up to around 105,000! The ground has hosted some really important games, including a European Cup and Champions League final, four Copa del Rey finals, Five World Cup matches, five UEFA Super Cups and 21 Spanish Super Cups!

O

OLYMPICS!

Another massively important event the Nou Camp's hosted was the 1992 Summer Olympics football tournament final! The city of Barcelona hosted the world famous sporting competition, with 95,000 supporters in attendance at the Nou Camp to watch Spain beat Poland 3-2 in the football final! Cadiz striker Kiko scored a last-minute winner!

P

PIQUE & PUYOL!

Picking two players for one letter isn't cheating – we promise! In fact, Gerard Pique and Carles Puyol had such a deep connection in central defence, they basically worked as one player anyway! They had a real 'Beauty and the Beast' partnership, with Puyol the passionate tough tackler and man mountain, and Pique the more elegant passer of the ball. It worked so well!

Q

QUINTUPLE!

Pep Guardiola was one of the finest midfielders to grace the Nou Camp, but he's also the most successful manager in the history of the club! He won 14 titles in his four-year spell as boss, with the 2008-09 season the most memorable. They came first in La Liga, lifted the Copa del Rey and Champions League, then won the Spanish Super Cup and UEFA Super Cup to seal a famous quintuple!

R

RONALDINHO!

Okay, so we might have already mentioned him in the Brazil category, but Ronaldinho deserves his own space! His incredible tekkers, no-look passes and deadly free-kicks made him a real fans' favourite during his five-year spell at the club. He even got applauded by Real Madrid supporters after scoring an amazing solo stunner at the Bernabeu in 2005!

S

STOICHKOV!

Striker Hristo Stoichkov was the hero of Bulgaria's shock run to the 1994 World Cup semi-finals, but he's fondly remembered as a Barcelona legend too! He scored 162 goals in 341 games for the club between 1990 and 1998, and in 1994 became only the third Barcelona player, after Johan Cruyff and Spain's Luis Suarez, to win the Ballon d'Or!

T

TIKI-TAKA!

As far as footballing philosophies go, Tiki-taka is up there with the best! The short passes and constant movement style of play originates from Johan Cruyff's Barcelona Dream Team in the early '90s, and was also used by Pep Guardiola when he was manager of the club. It's not just possession for the sake of it, though – you have to move forward with the ball too!

U

URRUTICOECHEA!

As well as having one of the trickiest names to spell, Javier Urruticoechea was also really difficult to score against! Considered as one of the club's best ever goalkeepers, 'Urruti' gained legendary status when he saved an all-important penalty against Real Valladolid in 1985 – it made sure Barça won the game and virtually sealed the Spanish championship!

V

VISCA!

Visca comes from the Catalan expression 'Visca Barça', which supporters shout to players to motivate them, and basically translates to 'Long live Barça'! Another common expression which you'll hear at the Nou Camp and see on the club's social media accounts is 'Força Barça', which means 'Come on Barça'! If you want to say it, remember the Catalan 'ç' is pronounced like an 's'!

W

WORLD CUP!

Spain might be the name on the 2010 World Cup trophy, but Barcelona fans will have felt proud of their players' involvement! Eight of their superstars were called up to Vicente del Bosque's squad, more than any other club, with seven academy products featuring in the final! Plus, Barcelona's own Andres Iniesta scored the winning goal!

X

XAVI!

The God of Tiki-taka, Xavi Hernandez is another absolute Barcelona legend. He's the only superstar to have played over 750 games for the club, and he did it during an epic career spanning 17 seasons! He was one of the best pinpoint passers the game will ever see – and he wasn't just a safe sideways passer either!

Y

YOUTH!

We've mentioned Barça's youth academy a few times in this A-Z, and La Masia is one of the best academies on the planet! It's a boarding school, where over 300 young talents go to live and learn to play the Barça way. It's also the only academy to have trained all three finalists for the Ballon d'Or in a single year – Andres Iniesta, Leo Messi and Xavi were the three nominees in 2010!

Z

ZAMORA!

Barcelona legend Ricardo Zamora, who played for La Blaugrana between 1919 and 1922, is regarded as one of the best keepers in history – and the award for the GK with the lowest goals-to-game ratio each La Liga season is named after him! Barça have won a record 20 Zamora Trophies, with Antoni Ramallets and Victor Valdes picking up five awards each!

WRITE YOUR OWN
BARCELONA A-Z

Fill in your own Barça A-Z and you could win a year's free subscription to MATCH magazine!

A. Academy

B. Ballon.d'Or

C. Clasico

D. De Jong

E. Espanyol

F. Femini

G. Joan Gamper

H. ~~Hymn~~ Hat-Tricks

I. Iniesta

J. Johan Cruyff

K. Kit

L. La ~~Blaugrana~~ Masia

M. Messi

N. Nou Camp

O. Olympics

P. Pedro

Q. Quality

R. Real Madrid

S. Supporters

T. Transfers

U. Urruticoechea

V. Visca

W. World Cup

X. Xavi

Y. YouTube

Z. Zamora

NAME: Claudia Bushby

DATE OF BIRTH: 23/11/07

ADDRESS: 39 Byron Mews, Hampstead, London NW32NQ

MOBILE: +44 7765 738418

EMAIL: claudiabushby@icloud...

BARCA'S BEST GOAL EVER!

Barcelona supporters have spoken – the debate is finally over. We now know the greatest goal in the club's long history!

HOW IT WORKED...

▶ Barcelona officials re-watched thousands of the club's best goals and made a shortlist of their favourites.
▶ They then put it to the fans to vote in a knockout format on the club's website – epic wondergoal v epic wondergoal!
▶ The votes were counted, and the winning goals progressed to the next round, until eventually there were four finalists...

THE WINNER!

Over 500,000 votes were cast, but the goal with the most support was Lionel Messi's Maradona-esque solo stunner v Getafe in 2007! He picked the ball up in his own half, skinned four defenders and rounded the keeper, before knocking the ball into the net with his weaker right foot!

Scan the QR code below to watch the goal and see Messi explain how it all happened...

Scan the QR code to watch these goals, too!

THE FINALISTS...

These were the other three goals that made it to the final four!

LIONEL MESSI
v ATHLETIC BILBAO, 2015

LIONEL MESSI
v REAL MADRID, 2011

SERGI ROBERTO
v PSG, 2017

We combine the skills of **BARCELONA**'s best ever players

HEADERS
ZLATAN IBRAHIMOVIC

Zlatan Ibrahimovic's two-year spell at Barcelona was actually a bit of a disaster, but one good thing to come from it is that we can use his DNA to form our Ultimate Player! We'd love to have his extreme confidence and tricks, but his height and heading ability would come in handy too!

YOU PICK: *Suarez*

REFLEXES
MARC-ANDRE TER STEGEN

Before you get confused, don't forget this is an Ultimate Player – he's got to be able to play in goal as well! Barça have had some incredible keepers throughout the years, like Andoni Zubizarreta and Victor Valdes, but just for his pure shot-stopping reflexes alone, we'd go for their current No.1!

YOU PICK: *ter Stegen*

DRIBBLING
LIONEL MESSI

If you want a dribbler that pulls off loads of cool tricks, go for Ronaldinho or Neymar, but if you want someone that's just impossible to win the ball off, it's got to be Diego Maradona or Lionel Messi – and we've gone for Leo! He'd probably be our pick for the best dribbler of all time, not just Barcelona's!

YOU PICK: *Lionel Messi*

PASSING
XAVI

We don't mean to be pushy, but surely you've got to pick Xavi for passing! He once completed 96 passes out of 96 in a Champions League match – a record high for completed CL passes in one match without giving the ball away! He was the ultimate symbol of Barcelona's tiki-taka style!

YOU PICK: *Puyol*

PLAYER!

to create an all-time superstar – and you can do the same!

VISION
ANDRES INIESTA

We reckon if you gave Spanish playmaker Andres Iniesta one of the world's toughest wordsearches, he'd find all the hidden words within a minute – his vision was that good! He always had his head up and knew exactly what was going on around him before picking out a killer through ball!

YOU PICK: Johan Cruyff

TACKLING
CARLES PUYOL

The ex-captain wasn't just a no-nonsense tackler, he was also a leader that was respected by every single one of his team-mates – and always gave everything he had for the club! The passion and hunger Puyol showed on the pitch is unrivalled by any player that's ever represented Barcelona!

YOU PICK: Gerard Pique.

SPEED
OUSMANE DEMBELE

We very almost picked current left-back Jordi Alba for this skill trait, but then we remembered that the lightning-quick Spanish international once admitted that Ousmane Dembele is quicker than him – so we had to go for the eye-catching France forward! His pace is absolutely electric!

YOU PICK: Joan Gamper

FINISHING
RONALDO

Okay, so he might have gone on to join massive rivals Real Madrid, but Ronaldo's goal-to-game ratio at Barcelona is better than the likes of Leo Messi, Luis Suarez or legend Laszlo Kubala – he scored 47 goals in 49 matches for the club! The Brazil icon was a total beast in front of goal!

YOU PICK: Antoine Griezmann

STAT ATTACK!

Get a load of BARÇA's biggest signings, longest winning streaks, record scorers, social media fans and tons more!

ALL-TIME APPEARANCES

	PLAYER	GAMES
1	Xavi	767
2	Lionel Messi	687
3	Andres Iniesta	674
4	Carles Puyol	594
5	Migueli	549

ALL-TIME TOP SCORERS

	PLAYER	GOALS
1	Lionel Messi	603
2	Cesar	232
3	Lazslo Kubala	194
4	Josep Samitier	184
5	Luis Suarez	177

6

In 2009-10, Pedro became the first player ever to score in six different official club competitions in one season!

Legendary goalkeeper **Victor Valdes** went 896 minutes without conceding a goal in all competitions in 2011-12 – a club record!

896

LA LIGA POSITION
LAST 20 SEASONS

1999-2000	2000-2001	2001-2002	2002-2003	2003-2004	2004-2005	2005-2006	2006-2007	2007-2008	2008-2009	2009-2010	2010-2011	2011-2012	2012-2013	2013-2014	2014-2015	2015-2016	2016-2017	2017-2018	2018-2019
2nd	4th	4th	6th	2nd	1st	1st	2nd	3rd	1st	1st	1st	2nd	1st	2nd	1st	1st	2nd	1st	1st

MAGIC MESSI!

LEO MESSI

Lionel Messi's 73 goals in all competitions in 2011-12 is a Blaugrana record for a single season – 50 of those came in La Liga!

13 COUNTRIES REPRESENTED IN 2018-19 SQUAD

Germany

Portugal | Spain | Croatia | France

Brazil | Uruguay | Argentina | Netherlands

Colombia | Ghana | Chile | Belgium

LA LIGA STREAKS!

LONGEST WINNING STREAK
16 matches

LONGEST UNBEATEN STREAK
43 matches

LONGEST SCORING STREAK
72 matches

LONGEST STRETCH AT TOP
59 matches

1998

Nike have been Barcelona's kit makers since 1998!

BIGGEST TRANSFERS

RECORD SIGNING
£107M
Antoine Griezmann from Atletico Madrid in 2019

RECORD SALE
£198M
Neymar to PSG in 2017

facebook
103+
MILLION Likes

72+
MILLION Likes

twitter
54+
MILLION Likes

Stats only include official matches. Correct up to the start of the 2019-20 season.

45

BARCA'S NEXT GENERATION!

We take a closer look at five of the hottest young footy talents ready to break through at the Nou Camp over the next couple of years!

RIQUI PUIG

MIDFIELDER

Puig isn't the strongest player in the Barça gym, but the likes of Messi, Iniesta and Xavi have already proven that you don't need to be big to be a huge success at the Nou Camp! He's got the technique, vision and decision-making to be a massive hit!

TOP SKILL: Vision

POTENTIAL
9
/10

POTENTIAL
8
/10

INAKI PENA

GOALKEEPER

Loads of Barcelona and Spanish experts reckon Pena can eventually take over from Marc-Andre ter Stegen between the Nou Camp sticks! He's a classic Cule keeper – he's just as good with his feet as he is with his hands!

TOP SKILL: Footwork

CARLES PEREZ

WINGER

Perez well and truly announced himself to Blaugrana fans after being promoted from the club's B team last summer – the ultra-direct dribbler bagged a goal on his first-ever senior start, then two assists the match after to rescue his side a point!

TOP SKILL: Dribbling

POTENTIAL
8
/10

POTENTIAL
10
/10

CARLES ALENA

MIDFIELDER

The classy midfielder was handed the No.19 jersey for 2019-20 – the same shirt number that Lionel Messi wore before he took on the famous No.10! We've got our fingers crossed Alena can have a similar career to the Argentina legend!

TOP SKILL: Creativity

ANSU FATI

WINGER

The teenage wing king, who turned down Real Madrid as a youngster, became Barça's youngest player in a competitive match for over 75 years when he made his league debut against Real Betis in August 2019, then became their youngest La Liga scorer the game after against Osasuna!

TOP SKILL: Shooting

POTENTIAL
9
/10

LEGENDS OF LA MASIA!

These five superstars proved it's possible to go from Barça's youth team to legendary Blaugrana ballers!

Lionel Messi

Barça believed so much in the 13-year-old Messi's footy talents, they used to pay £1,000 a month for his growth hormone treatment!

Andres Iniesta

Iniesta said he sobbed for days when his parents first left him at La Masia, and he cried again after playing his last game for the club in 2018!

Xavi

We can't imagine how many games of keep-ball Xavi must have played as a kid at La Masia to become such a perfect pinpoint passer!

Carles Puyol

Even when he was at La Masia, Puyol was known for his long curly locks, incredible leadership and top tackling tekkers!

Sergio Busquets

Busquets was promoted from the Barça B team over ten years ago by Pep Guardiola – another top La Masia product!

CROSSWORD

Use the clues to fill in this tricky Barcelona crossword puzzle!

ACROSS

4. Asian country that Andres Iniesta moved to when he left Barcelona in 2018! (5)

6. Legendary ex-player and manager, Johan _ _ _ _ _ _! (6)

7. Position that Barça legend Samuel Eto'o used to play! (7)

8. Complete the club's motto – Mes que un _ _ _ _! (4)

11. Surname of ex-goal king, Zlatan _ _ _ _ _ _ _ _ _ _! (11)

13. The club Barcelona signed Jordi Alba from in 2012! (8)

15. One of their awesome nicknames! (2,9)

18. The number of Brazilian players in their first-team squad in 2018-19! (4)

20. Country that full-back Nelson Semedo is from! (8)

DOWN

1. Main colour of their third shirt in 2018-19! (4)

2. The three letters that serve as the club's abbreviation! (3)

3. Name of their second-highest La Liga goalscorer in the 2018-19 season! (4,6)

5. The team Barça finished directly above in La Liga in 2018-19! (8,6)

9. Shirt number that total legend Xavi used to wear! (3)

10. Mega brand that produces Barcelona's wicked kits! (4)

12. English team that knocked Barcelona out of the 2018-19 Champions League! (9)

14. English club that Barça Femeni signed ex-star Toni Duggan from in 2017! (3,4)

16. Name of their world-famous academy! (2,5)

17. French club that Barcelona Femeni lost to in the 2018-19 Champions League final! (4)

19. Mega boot brand that Luis Suarez loves to wear! (4)

NAME THE TEAM

Can you remember the superstars that lined up in Barcelona's 3-0 Champions League victory over Man. United in 2018-19?

1. Goalkeeper
ter Stegen

2. Centre-back
Lenglet

3. Midfielder
Ivan Rakitic

4. Def. midfielder
Sergio Busquets

5. Centre-back
Gerard Pique

6. Forward
Lionel Messi

7. Right-back
Sergio Roberto

8. Midfielder
Arthur

9. Forward
Coutinho Coutinho

10. Striker
Suarez

11. Left-back
Alba

ANSWERS ON PAGE 60

CLUB HISTORY

Flick through the Barça history books!

BARCELONA THROUGH THE YEARS!

BARÇA'S BIRTH!

Shortly after arriving in Barcelona from Switzerland, sports fanatic Joan Gamper decided to form a Footy team. In October 1899, he put an advert in a local newspaper, and a month later had a squad of 12 players from Germany, Switzerland, Spain and even two Englishmen! It was from that moment that FC Barcelona was born!

FIRST EL CLASICO!

The year 1902 was one to remember for Barça fans! Not only did they win their first ever trophy – the Copa Macaya, contested between Catalan clubs – they also won the First El Clasico in history! The game was played in Madrid and Real went ahead, but Barça came back to win 3-1!

1902

LA LIGA DEBUT!

The 1920s was a golden age for Barça – they opened a new 22,000-capacity ground, had over 10,000 members and players like Ricardo Zamora and Paulino Alcantara had become superstars! They reached a new peak in 1929 though, winning the first ever La Liga season – finishing two points above Real!

1929

1910

1899

1949

At the beginning, Barça's shirt was half blue and half claret, while the shorts were white. The most likely theory behind the original kit is that it came from the rugby team where two of the club's English members had studied in their youth!

CLUB CREST!

Originally, Gamper and co. had chosen to use the same badge as the city of Barcelona, but decided they needed their own in 1910. They organised a competition to find a new design, and the winning one is more or less the same as the crest that's used today!

LATIN CUP CHAMPS!

Barcelona marked their 50th anniversary by winning their first ever European trophy – the 1949 Latin Cup! Organised by FIFA, it was contested by the league champions from Spain, Portugal, Italy and France, with Barça beating Sporting 2-1 in the final!

'BARÇA OF FIVE CUPS'!

The 1951-52 season was so special for Barça – they won five trophies, including La Liga, the Latin Cup, Spanish Cup, Copa Eva Duarte and Copa Martini & Rossi! Their squad had the club's second and third all-time top scorers – Cesar and Lazslo Kubala!

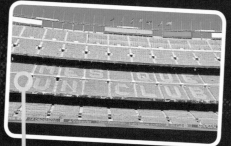

75TH ANNIVERSARY!

Barcelona's 75th anniversary was a big celebration – especially as the club had just won the La Liga title! It was also the birth of 'El Cant del Barça', their famous official hymn, which was created to mark the epic milestone!

MES QUE UN CLUB!

Incoming Barça president Narcis de Carreras gave an acceptance speech in January 1968, saying that Barcelona was 'mes que un club' – or 'more than a football club'. It's from there that the famous motto was born, and it can still be found on the seats at the Nou Camp!

1974

1968

1973

1982

1952

1957
NOU CAMP OPENS!

Work started in 1954 to build Barça's new ground – and three years later the Nou Camp was opened. With an initial capacity of 99,053 spectators, fans flocked to see the first ever game there – Barça beat Polish side Warsaw 4-2, with Paraguayan striker Eulogio Martinez scoring the first goal!

MARADONA MOVE!

Barça broke the world transfer record again to bring Argentina legend Diego Maradona to the club in 1982! He produced some special moments, and became the first star in the modern era to break the world transfer record twice when he joined Napoli in 1984!

CRUYFF ARRIVES: PART 1!

In 1973, Barça signed Johan Cruyff from Ajax for a world-record transfer fee! In his first season, he helped Barcelona end their 14-year wait for a league trophy, and starred in the club's 5-0 thrashing of Real Madrid at the Bernabeu! He went on to lift the Ballon d'Or in 1974, too!

RIJKAARD & RONALDINHO!

In the summer of 2003, Barcelona had a shake-up, with Frank Rijkaard joining as coach and making Ronaldinho his marquee signing! Things turned out perfectly, as Barça won the 2004-05 La Liga title, then the league and Champions League double the season after – beating Arsenal 2-1 in the 2006 final in Paris!

BALLON D'OR BALLERS!

In 2010, Barça made history by becoming the first team to have three academy players make the top three of the Ballon d'Or awards – Lionel Messi, Andres Iniesta and Xavi!

2010

CRUYFF ARRIVES: PART 2!

Ten years after leaving Barça as a player, Cruyff returned as manager – and his impact was incredible! During his reign he formed the 'Dream Team', which won the club's first-ever European Cup in 1992 at Wembley against Sampdoria! He also lifted four La Liga trophies in a row between 1991 and 1994!

2003

2009

1988

1999

2000

MESSI SIGNS!

In September 2000, a 13-year-old Leo Messi arrived in Barcelona with his family to show off his talents. Three months later, the club's technical secretary decided to seal the deal with the player's agent – signing an initial contract on a napkin in the club's canteen!

CENTURY CELEBRATIONS!

In order to mark 100 years as a club, Barcelona put on a series of events at the end of November in 1999 – including a massive fiesta in the Nou Camp with around 100,000 fans in attendance!

PERFECT PEP!

Ex-hero Pep Guardiola returned to the first team as gaffer in 2008, and in 2009 he won six trophies! As well as winning La Liga, the Copa del Rey, UEFA Super Cup, Spanish Super Cup and FIFA Club World Cup, they beat Man. United 2-0 in the 2009 Champions League final!

WEMBLEY AGAIN!

Johan Cruyff and co. had won the club's first ever European Cup at England's national stadium, and the team of 2010-11 created more happy memories there by beating Man. United 3-1 in the 2011 CL final, including goals by Pedro, David Villa and Messi!

COMEBACK KINGS!

The Nou Camp witnessed one of the most remarkable European games ever in 2017! Barça had lost their quarter-final first-leg clash with PSG 4-0 in Paris, but somehow managed to win 6-1 in the return leg, including two stoppage-time net-busters!

2017

2011

2019

2015

LA LIGA LEGENDS!

After almost going the whole La Liga season unbeaten in their jaw-dropping 2017-18 campaign, Barça followed it up by winning back-to-back titles – and finishing a record 19 points above Clasico rivals Real Madrid in 2018-19!

HISTORY MAKERS!

Another ex-Barcelona midfielder took over in 2014 – Luis Enrique – and a year later he was celebrating La Blaugrana becoming the first European team ever to bag two continental trebles, beating Juventus 3-1 in the Champions League final in Berlin!

EL CLASICO HEROES!

We've picked out five stars that have a history of embarrassing Real Madrid – something BARCELONA fans are very happy about!

5 DIEGO MARADONA

FAB FACT!
Maradona scored 22 goals in just 36 league games during his two-year spell at the Nou Camp!

He might have only played a handful of Clasicos, but Argentina legend Diego Maradona provided a moment of pure brilliance back in 1983. In the first leg of Spain's old Copa de la Liga final at the Santiago Bernabeu, he received a through ball, rounded the keeper and then skinned another defender on the goal line – who went crashing into the post! Some Madrid fans even stood up to applaud the goal!

EL CLASICO STATS

GAMES	5	WINS	3	GOALS	3

4 GARY LINEKER

FAB FACT!
Barça paid £2.8 million to sign Lineker back in 1986. Absolute bargain!

The ex-Three Lions goal machine joined Barcelona on the back of winning the 1986 World Cup Golden Boot, and he adjusted super quickly to life in Spain. He scored 20 goals in just 41 league games in his first season, which included his most memorable moment in a Barça shirt! In just his second Clasico, he scored a stunning hat-trick in an awesome 3-2 win against the eventual league champions at the Nou Camp!

EL CLASICO STATS

GAMES	8	WINS	4	GOALS	5

EL CLASICO VILLAINS!

Check out these five El Clasico villains, too. Boo!

ALFREDO DI STEFANO

The legendary attacker nearly joined Barcelona in 1953, but ended up at Real Madrid instead – and scored 18 goals against Los Cules!

CRISTIANO RONALDO

Cristiano equalled Di Stefano's El Clasico record in May 2018 to become Real's joint all-time top scorer against Barcelona with 18 goals!

3 LUIS SUAREZ

FAB FACT!
Suarez has scored against Real Madrid in every season since joining Barça in 2014!

Barcelona's third-highest goalscorer in El Clasico history has bagged some important goals against their arch rivals – none more so than his jaw-dropping hat-trick in 2018-19, which saw his side thump Real Madrid 5-1 at the Nou Camp without star man Lionel Messi! He also netted the winner against Los Blancos in his first season at the club in 2014-15, helping Los Cules regain the La Liga title in the process. Hero!

EL CLASICO STATS

GAMES		WINS		GOALS	
	14		7		11

2 RONALDINHO

FAB FACT!
Just over a week after his Bernabeu heroics, Ronaldinho won the 2005 Ballon d'Or award!

In November 2005, Barça and Real were separated by just one point in the La Liga table and were about to face-off in a mega clash at the Santiago Bernabeu. Samuel Eto'o put Los Cules ahead, but the second half was simply the 'Ronaldinho Show'. He scored a solo stunner in the 60th minute, before repeating the feat 17 minutes later to seal the win – and even had the Real Madrid supporters on their feet clapping him!

EL CLASICO STATS

GAMES		WINS		GOALS	
	8		3		5

1 LIONEL MESSI

FAB FACT!
Leo's epic winner in 2017 was his 500th goal in a Barça shirt!

El Clasico's all-time top scorer provided one of the most iconic Real-Barça moments in April 2017 at the Bernabeu. Barcelona were 2-1 ahead with Sergio Ramos sent off, before James Rodriguez scored an 85th-minute equaliser. Messi had the last laugh, though – he scored the winner in the 93rd minute, and celebrated by taking off his shirt and holding it up in front of the home fans!

EL CLASICO STATS

GAMES		WINS		GOALS	
	41		19		26

LUIS FIGO

The Portugal winger was a massive fans' favourite at the Nou Camp... that's until he joined Real in 2000 and became an arch enemy!

RAUL

The all-time Spanish legend celebrated a goal at the Nou Camp in 1999 by putting his finger to his lips and telling the crowd to be quiet!

JOSE MOURINHO

Jose used to work as a translator for Barça, but became one of their most hated figures when he took over as Madrid coach!

2019-20 FIRST TEAM SQUAD

GOALKEEPERS

No.	Player		La Liga Games/Goals 2018-19	Signed from
1	Marc-Andre ter Stegen		35/0	B. M'gladbach, 2014
13	Neto		34/0	Valencia, 2019

Neto

DEFENDERS

No.	Player		La Liga Games/Goals 2018-19	Signed from
2	Nelson Semedo		26/1	Benfica, 2017
3	Gerard Pique		35/4	Man. United, 2008
6	Jean-Clair Todibo		2/0	Toulouse, 2019
15	Clement Lenglet		23/1	Sevilla, 2018
16	Moussa Wague		3/0	Eupen, 2018
18	Jordi Alba		36/2	Valencia, 2012
23	Samuel Umtiti		14/0	Lyon, 2016
24	Junior Firpo		24/3	Real Betis, 2019

Todibo

MIDFIELDERS

No.	Player		La Liga Games/Goals 2018-19	Signed from
4	Ivan Rakitic		34/3	Sevilla, 2014
5	Sergio Busquets		35/0	Academy
8	Arthur		27/0	Gremio, 2018
19	Carles Alena		17/2	Academy
20	Sergi Roberto		29/0	Academy
21	Frenkie de Jong		N/A	Ajax, 2019
22	Arturo Vidal		33/3	Bayern Munich, 2018

Griezmann

FORWARDS

No.	Player		La Liga Games/Goals 2018-19	Signed from
9	Luis Suarez		33/21	Liverpool, 2014
10	Lionel Messi		34/36	Academy
11	Ousmane Dembele		29/8	B. Dortmund, 2017
17	Antoine Griezmann		37/15	Atletico Madrid, 2019

MEET THE MANAGER

ERNESTO VALVERDE

Get the complete lowdown on the gaffer in charge of BARCELONA...

RECORD BREAKER!

After becoming Barcelona boss in May 2017, his spell in charge started terribly – they lost both legs of their Spanish Super Cup clash v Real Madrid! It certainly wasn't a sign of things to come, though – they ended 2017-18 as double winners and became the first La Liga side in history to go 43 games without defeat!

LA LIGA CHAMP!

After winning La Liga in 2017-18, the pressure was on Valverde to maintain his sick start and claim back-to-back league titles amid pressure from arch rivals Real and Atletico Madrid. They might have faltered in the CL but, once again, Valverde's boys were too strong in La Liga, winning the 2018-19 title by 11 points. Campeones!

DONE DEAL!

In February 2019, Los Cules chiefs offered boss Valverde a one-year contract extension until the end of the 2019-20 campaign, with the option to extend it for a further season. Valverde signed on the dotted line straight away and will now be aiming for a hat-trick of Spanish league titles in 2019-20!

"Valverde seems to me to be a spectacular coach beyond the friendship that unites us. He has done a very good job!"
Pep Guardiola, ex-Barcelona player and manager

PAST PLAYER!

Before becoming the manager, Valverde spent two years at Barça as a player. The ex-forward was at the Nou Camp from 1988 to 1990, playing 22 league games and scoring eight goals. He was also part of the squads that lifted the 1989 European Cup Winners' Cup and the 1990 Copa del Rey – he's got Barcelona in his blood!

STAT ATTACK!

Take a look at some of Valverde's epic stats since taking over...

 **109**
At the end of 2018-19, midfielder Ivan Rakitic had been picked the most by Valverde in all competitions!

 6
After losing his first two games v Real Madrid as Barça boss, he then went on an ace six-match unbeaten run in El Clasico!

 80
Barcelona won 80 of their first 115 games in all comps under Valverde, losing just ten of those matches!

 274
During that same time period, Barça scored 274 goals in all competitions – averaging well over two per game!

BARCELONA FEMENI
ultimate guide!

The **BARCELONA WOMEN'S** team is one of the best in Europe! Here's what makes them so special...

EUROPEAN RUNNERS-UP

Lyon might have beaten them 4-1 in the 2019 Women's Champions League final, but Barcelona still made history by reaching their first ever European final. After losing their last 32 first leg 3-1 to BIIK Kazygurt of Kazakhstan, Barça Femeni totally turned things around and went on to win seven Champions League matches in a row without conceding a goal, scoring 17 along the way!

LEAGUE LEGENDS

Athletic Bilbao have won the most Spanish Women's Primera Division titles with five, but Barcelona Femeni are the only club to have won four back-to-back league trophies and hold the record for most points in a single season. They bagged an incredible 94 in 2011-12, winning 31 out of 34 games, and scored a whopping 119 goals!

WORLD CUP WONDERS

The 2019 Women's World Cup was a great event, and Barça Femeni fans got to see loads of their stars in action. The 15 Blaugrana players called up, including ten in Spain's squad, were more than any club in the world – and that didn't include Norway's Caroline Graham Hansen, who officially became a Barça player halfway through the tournament!

RECORD BREAKERS

When Barcelona Femeni played eventual league champions Atletico Madrid at the Wanda Metropolitano in March 2019, 60,739 supporters were in attendance – a world record for a top-flight women's domestic football game! Barcelona fans were in for a real treat, too – Asisat Oshoala and Toni Duggan both netted to give Los Cules a memorable 2-0 victory!

TONI DUGGAN

England forward Toni Duggan was only the fourth Brit to play for Barcelona, and the first ever English player to star for their Femeni side. She moved to Spain in 2017 after winning the FA Women's Super League with Man. City the previous year, and ended up scoring 20 goals in just 51 league games before leaving the club following the 2019 Women's World Cup!

5 stars to watch!

We've picked out five Barcelona Femeni superstars to keep an eye out for in 2020...

Sandra Panos
Goalkeeper

Panos let in just 11 goals in 27 matches in 2018-19 – the lowest goals-to-game ratio in the league!

Vicky Losada
Midfielder

The captain's won loads of trophies with Barça Femeni, and she's also played for Arsenal!

Alexia Putellas
Midfielder

She's played over 200 games for Barça since joining in 2012, and was top scorer in 2018-19!

Asisat Oshoala
Forward

The ex-Arsenal forward signed on a permanent deal in May 2019 after impressing on loan!

Lieke Martens
Forward

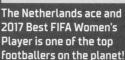

The Netherlands ace and 2017 Best FIFA Women's Player is one of the top footballers on the planet!

barcelona... the club!

Check out some of the other top sports Barça has teams for...

Roller Hockey
Barcelona's roller hockey team is the most successful in both Spain and Europe!

Futsal
They had five Brazilians in their awesome futsal side in 2018-19. Samba skills!

Handball
The handball team has lifted the most trophies in Spain and Europe, too. Legends!

Beach Soccer
They also have successful clubs in beach soccer, rugby, volleyball and basketball!

Wordfit — P16

Brain-Buster — P30

1. Sergio Busquets
2. True
3. Bordeaux
4. Barcelona
5. Barcelona 6-1 Real Madrid
6. 2017
7. Marc-Andre ter Stegen
8. No.18
9. Second
10. Gerard Pique

Name The Team — P49

1. Marc-Andre ter Stegen
2. Clement Lenglet
3. Ivan Rakitic
4. Sergio Busquets
5. Gerard Pique
6. Lionel Messi
7. Sergi Roberto
8. Arthur
9. Philippe Coutinho
10. Luis Suarez
11. Jordi Alba

Spot The Difference — P17

Crossword — P48

Face In The Crowd — P31

ROLL OF HONOUR

CHAMPIONS LEAGUE
1991-92, 2005-06, 2008-09, 2010-11, 2014-15

FIFA CLUB WORLD CUP
2009, 2011, 2015

EUROPEAN CUP WINNERS' CUP
1978-79, 1981-82, 1988-89, 1996-97

FAIRS CUP
1957-58, 1959-60, 1965-66 (won outright in 1971)

EUROPEAN SUPER CUP
1992, 1997, 2009, 2011, 2015

LA LIGA
1928-29, 1944-45, 1947-48, 1948-49, 1951-52, 1952-53,
1958-59, 1959-60, 1973-74, 1984-85, 1990-91, 1991-92,
1992-93, 1993-94, 1997-98, 1998-99, 2004-05, 2005-06,
2008-09, 2009-10, 2010-11, 2012-13, 2014-15, 2015-16,
2017-18, 2018-19

COPA DEL REY
1909-10, 1911-12, 1912-13, 1919-20, 1921-22, 1924-25, 1925-26,
1927-28, 1941-42, 1950-51, 1951-52, 1952-53, 1956-57, 1958-59,
1962-63, 1967-68, 1970-71, 1977-78, 1980-81, 1982-83,
1987-88, 1989-90, 1996-97, 1997-98, 2008-09,
2011-12, 2014-15, 2015-16, 2016-17, 2017-18

SPANISH SUPER CUP
1983, 1991, 1992, 1994, 1996, 2005, 2006, 2009,
2010, 2011, 2013, 2016, 2018

SPANISH LEAGUE CUP
1982-83, 1985-86

SMALL WORLD CUP
1957

LATIN CUP
1949, 1952

PYRENEES CUP
1910, 1911, 1912, 1913

MEDITERRANEAN LEAGUE
1937

CATALAN LEAGUE
1937-38

CATALAN LEAGUE CHAMPIONSHIP
1901-02, 1902-03, 1904-05, 1908-09, 1909-10, 1910-11,
1912-13, 1915-16, 1918-19, 1919-20, 1920-21, 1921-22, 1923-24,
1924-25, 1925-26, 1926-27, 1927-28, 1929-30, 1930-31,
1931-32, 1934-35, 1935-36, 1937-38 (includes Copa
Macaya 1901-02 & Copa Barcelona 1902-03)

CATALAN SUPER CUP
2014-15

CATALAN CUP
1990-91, 1992-93, 1999-2000, 2003-04, 2004-05, 2006-07,
2012-13, 2013-14 (until 1993-94, Copa Generalitat)

COPA EVA DUARTE
1948-49, 1951-52, 1952-53